Once I Gazed at You in Wonder

Once
I Gazed at You
in Wonder

Poems

JAN
HELLER
LEVI

Louisiana State University Press
Baton Rouge
1999

This book would not have been possible without the faith, support, and encouragement of Donna Masini, Ken Sofer, Linda Collins, Carol Conroy, Jane Cooper, Rochelle Feinstein, June Jordan, Christoph Keller, Cherryl Llewellyn, Micki Trager, Jonathan Santlofer, Nancy Steel and Tom Huhn, Jane and Michael Stern, Kim Vaeth, and the colony of Yaddo. It enters the world with my great thanks to Alice Fulton.

Designer: Melanie O'Quinn Samaha
Typeface: Sabon, Gill Sans
Printer and binder: Edwards Brothers, Inc.

Library of Congress Cataloging-in-Publication Data
Levi, Jan Heller.
    Once I gazed at you in wonder : Jan Heller Levi.
    p. cm.
    ISBN 0-8071-2364-1 (cloth : alk. paper). —ISBN 0-8071-2365-X
(paper : alk. paper)
    I. Title.
PS3562.E8877053   1999
811'.54—dc21   98-50182
                                            CIP

The author gratefully acknowledges the editors and staffs of the following publications, in which some of the poems herein, or versions of them, first appeared: *Antioch Review:* "Sex Is Not Important"; *Beloit Poetry Journal:* "Baltimore"; *Embers:* "Just as That Night," "Moonstone"; *Graham House Review:* "The Second Movement of Anything"; *Iowa Review:* "Formal Feeling: A Sequence"; *New Orleans Review:* "Halfway"; *Pequod:* "Some Other Where"; *Ploughshares* (Vol. 15, No. 4): "In Trouble"; *Poetry East:* "Conversation"; *River Styx:* "A Day"; *St. Galler Tagblatt:* "I walk back and forth in my room. . . ." (in translation); *Sojourner:* "Tuscarora."

In memory of Muriel Rukeyser,
Katrina Trask and her lost children,
and my mother

I

II

III

IV

V

VI

I

In Trouble

I can put her in an airplane;
I can put him in a window seat.
I can put clouds beneath the wings,
like wrinkled pajama tops, like
Toni permanent waves, like wave
after wave of cornfield in Minnesota,
where she's from. No,
him. I can have her smiling
when she hands him a drink, I can
make her eyes blue,
though mine are brown.

Or I can put him in an emergency room,
put her in the hallway.
I can wrap a strip of gauze
around her finger. I can
make it throb. I can
offer his smile to her,
I can give them one umbrella
to share, it's only drizzling,
all the way to her apartment.
No, his. I can give them
small talk, give her voice
a rhythm, his another,
keep them talking
till the rhythms match.
I can put a pillow on his couch,
give it tassels she likes
the feel of, slipping through her fingers.
I can give her lips like mine,
give her his lips on them.
I can nurse him at her breast.
I can kiss the nipples pink.
Then I can make a telephone cord,

very thick and very black,
wrap around her wrist
as she calls to say she's
in trouble.

I can hear him say, "I have a friend—"
can remind myself it's 1953, so he
probably doesn't.
I can put her in her apartment, December,
January, February, listening to Bach
because each note throbs sad
and perfect in her belly.
Then I can put her at a window, make
her watch the trees fill up with leaves.
I can make that little fish swim in salt,
can let it know each turn, each spin,
is a perfect sadness. I can kick and know
each time I kick she sucks
in her breath and hates.

I can make it take twelve hours,
can make it burn, or I can make it easy,
give her a nurse to brush
the damp hair off her face.
I can make the lighting stark or gauzy,
I can make her feel real proud, or dead,
real dead inside,
when the cord is cut, and when I cry.
For the first time. The only time.

I can make the wheels of the gurney squeak
when they roll her out.
I can make it that way, make it so
the womb glides out, I can put the slick
and bloody thing in a doctor's hands.
I don't need you,
she tells herself.

I can make her say that;
make her say you,
not her, not it.
Or I can make her give me a name, Priscilla,
that's pretty, or Angela,
she's always liked that.

I can make her fingers slender.
I can make them uncurl, I can make a moment
when I hover in space before falling
from her hands, giving,
into their hands, taking.
I can make her forget.
I can make her never forget.
I can put myself on a nubby, violet couch,
can put a palm and gentle fingers on my forehead,
I can have that hand—
my mother's hand—
pushing the hair off my face, again
and again, as she tells me the story
that has none of this.
I can make my eyes open when she tells me the story.
I can make my eyes close when she tells me the story.
I can make my eyes close.

Sex Is Not Important

1.

Sex is not important. That's why
we have conversation. In the dark,
the unforgivable dark, it's hope
that's important, and hope
is something I do alone.

2.

So here comes the unfortunate part.
Sisters /*Brothers*/, forgive me:
what we always love about the other
man /*woman*/ is that she /*he*/ doesn't
care;
he's got an itch he's going to scratch;
she's going to lick you like a puppy
hungry for your salt;
he's going to cry out and he's going to fall,
sweating and flushed and finished,
beside your trembling.
She's going to keep her eyes open and her mouth shut.
And he's going to leave you, not knowing what he's left.

3.

It's not your body, is it,
that glows in the night,
and it's not me,
that woman in that hotel room,
doing all that wanting?

It can't be. I'm too smart
for all this;
too smart to disturb

these hospital corners
with this unaccountable thrashing.

It must be my mind.
It's oozing.
It's evaluated the situation
and suggested
that my back should arch,
arch, arch. Oh!,

you're so *interesting*.
When we're ourselves
again, we really should
talk about this.

Have you ever seen
those teenagers clenched
on street corners,
repetitively touching lips?
I think it's because
they have nothing to say.

But you and I
have so much in common:
this, for example,
and that.

4.

Sex is not important. That's why
we have everything else: friends,
husbands, work, books, politics,
postcards, art, and poetry.
That's why, when the telephone rings,
we answer. That's why
we wake up in the morning,
sick to our stomach with dreams,
and ready to live.

5.

That's why I have my circle game:
no one here but me and my abstract fame.

Everything unspoken
an endearment.

A woman's nipple—mine—

finds a finger.

My Father Calls Me Every Sunday Morning

My father calls me every Sunday morning.
Floating up out of sleep,
I can feel it coming.
He's been awake for hours.
He checks his watch,
pulls the phone onto his lap
like a recalcitrant child,
punches his Sprint code into its dumb face.
Lying in bed, I can feel each note—clear, blue as a vein—
pulsing;
through 200 miles of tense wire, my father's idea
of fatherhood speeding toward me.
And every Sunday it explodes,
precisely on schedule,
in the black box nailed to my wall.

We start with the weather: what it's doing up here,
what it's doing down there.
My father knows: everything of consequence
happens first in Baltimore, consequently
elsewhere. He instructs me on storms,
cold fronts, travel advisories, heading steadily my way.
What does he want? I've learned one trick.
I tell him a story—almost any will do—
as long as I've done or said something in it
that makes me sound like a fool.
This always works.
My father laughs.
His laugh is gorgeous.
It starts from somewhere
deep in his chest, billows up and up into the world.

When you hear it, you think of a man
striding through deep woods,

swinging his arms in the wintergreen air.
And hearing that laugh, the rise
and the rise of it,
I love him so madly. Like the tree
loves the man who comes to fell her,
her long awful groan
as she goes reeling toward earth
indistinguishable
from the lumberjack's
long roar of delight.

Best Cup of Coffee in Town

The forecast? Cool & sunny, with scattered
showers. It's 90, not a sign of rain. **Bam!**
The subway doors (well, some at least) slam
open. We squeeze, squeeze tighter, then splatter

across the platform, roll like a sweaty
wave toward the exit sign for 7th Avenue.
We break & scatter once we hit—fooled
again!—the steamy shores of 6th. Be-

neath, of course, some busted neon, winking:
**5th Avenue Coffee Shop—Home of the Best
Cup of Coffee in Town.** Weary waitress,
once I'm inside, taps her foot. I'm thinking:

which should it be? The mountain of golden brown
french fries? Or the mouth-watering cantaloupe
with the farm-fresh cottage cheese? I ask for both,
please. MyNameIsNancyHaveANiceDay frowns,

& disappears. It's true that this city
has changed me. Ten years ago, I was more
something than I am now. But I'm sure
I am still, despite it all, a pretty

good person. How else to explain my waking,
four days out of seven, feeling lousy: why
did I tell A I'd phone in an hour when I knew
I'd wait two? Why pat B's shaking

hand & coo I know just what you mean,
when I didn't? And why, just last evening,
did I say terrific! re: C's sestina,
when it was just in lines 12 & 16

that a handful of words broke free, prying
themselves off the page & into my tired heart?
I keep telling myself: (1) don't be so hard
on yourself, (2) you're simply trying

not to hurt anyone's feelings, & (3)
wouldn't this world be gruesome if we all
said what we really mean? Really awful:
everyone a poet, singing his or her squeaky,

honest song? How would we get anything done?
Still, I suppose I've got to draw
the line somewhere. Why not here? "Miss!" I call.
She lifts her sad head sadly. "Yeah, hon?"

"This coffee," I growl, pointing down to the thin,
muddy swirl, "this is—" "Is what?" she sighs.
Her teeth are the same familiar & dull white
as the I ♥ New York button pinned

to her chest. She looks like she's had it up
to here with the truth. And she also looks a bit
brave & sweet, waiting there, for some more of it.
"Is delicious," I say. "I'll take another cup."

Some Other Where

Tut, I have lost myself, I am not here;
This is not Romeo, he's some other where.

Even the most stony heart of a 29-year-old woman who has
passed her time for suicide
feels lonely, lost, and too bourgeois at the sight
of Juliet's balcony; at the soaring, crumbled façade
of the home that they call Romeo's.
I buy a postcard. My neck cranks up
like a rusty crane. Wet leaves tumble down a pink wall.

No woman in her right mind visits Verona with her in-laws.
They balk at the admission price:
"Oh, what's to see? An empty house? Maybe a bed?"

Sucker for formula watercolors of the Canal of Sighs
and plaster pietàs (eight days in a rented Fiat,
we've ripped through Italy like Hitler through Poland),
my husband's mother suddenly becomes a scholar:

"I think Shakespeare made the whole thing up."

But they killed themselves!
(or he said they did, it's just the same)
at the highest heights of love;
never grew together,
to bicker and mumble down these most beautiful streets,
of roughage, calluses, and
"Michelin says you can see the whole city in an hour and a half."

Oh, where is Romeo?
Ken, resting back at the pensione, with a slight fever.
Maybe diarrhea.

Conversation

Wind chimes.

A mobile of cut glass.

A slice of eye in one, the tick beneath the dog's fur in another.
You save letters, but you never reread them.

I know. This one calls that one, that one drinks martinis
down at the seaport.

You burned the ticks. They sizzled, then exploded.

Antigone said, I dared. It was not God's proclamation.
One of their favorite photographs was taken just a few
months before she died.

Already the cancer made her smile differently. Creases
in her face that hadn't been there a year before. So much effort
to smile. But there was always so much effort in her smile, no one
seemed to notice the extra effort.

True, they don't mention it.

What they do say: She would have wanted this. She would
have said that. How do they know? She's spinning out there.

Once upon a time, many families slept with the windows wide open.
In the mornings your father and his brother shoveled the snow
out of their bedroom. To love him, it's easiest for you
to think of him thirteen, leaning into the cold work.

Why say it that way? My father was cold. He shoveled.
I love him. Once my uncle turned over a dinner plate, pressed
his finger to the words printed there, and said, priceless.

Sometimes a yellow line, sometimes a pale blue, sometimes a pink, lights up a page. That's what you think.

I don't want that. I want this. No, I don't want this. I want that. The worst thing I can think of is saying something and having the other person, no matter how hard you try to explain, completely miss the point.

Why?

Isn't it obvious?

I don't know.

But it's obvious.

No, it isn't.

There, you see. Look how mean the stars have always been to me, always blinking. I like swimming against the current, but only because it makes me feel I've earned the ease and pleasure of floating back to where I started.

You were happy. Remember the pale purple couch in the den? You stretched out on it and watched TV. *Father Knows Best.* *Lassie.* You were crazy about that dog—

I like the idea of things more than things themselves.

No. You like the residue of ideas. Loose threads. The paint that goes beyond the border of the canvas. The sulfur sting after you extinguish the match. When you were little, you could never crayon inside the lines.

They seemed so arbitrary.

The amethyst ring slipped off your finger.

Yes.

And into the toilet.

Yes. It was very beautiful, swirling down. It clinked
a few times against the porcelain. I remember the sound.

You like a dress that's too big. Because it makes you look
slight within its bigness. As though you might be pregnant,
but you're not, because look at your neck, your wrists,
they're so slender.

And the definite colors of sunset.

Recently, you've lost the knack of talking on the phone.
This is not tragic.

I saw a young woman and her mother crossing 1st Avenue,
holding hands and laughing.

Listen, it doesn't matter what season it is when you stand
in a cemetery, gathered around an arrangement of dirt
that no one goes too near.

It was fall.

Sometimes the birds sound like windshield wipers.
As you grow older, you love more.

Yes. Look at this.

For how long?

Until you can't bear to look at it anymore.

Ok, I'm finished.

Thank you. Thank you for trying. Thank you for opera,
little pools of light on the sidewalk. Thank you for 1957.
Thank you for that instant when he said he felt nothing,
and I knew he was lying.

And for her skin. It was so soft and really she had the most
beautiful hands. And laughing! Crossing 1st Avenue and laughing!

II

Marjory Heller Weinberg Levi
(1917–1978)

*And soon all of us will sleep under the earth, we
who never let each other sleep above it.*
—*Marina Tsvetaeva*

Formal Feeling: A Sequence

Formal Feeling

1.

September. The rabbi didn't know her.
All day I expect her, look for her in every room.
I have so much to tell her now.

Orange strands from the carpet cling to my feet.

Where is she?
Where is she?

2.

Now let me tell you about minutes of lead,
the color blue. Blue is the color of her
fingernails, her lips, my father's wet eyes.
Blue is the color of some other world I insist
she sees. Blue is their language, their children,
their future, dissolving.

Now let me tell you what we can tell the dying:
nothing.

Now let me tell you about a kingdom, about transformations,
about a healing, about a radio turned full volume
for which she would not turn her head.

8:40. 8:41.
I begin the slow, proud walk into motherless America.

3.

October. Now I dream
dreams of perfect love and almost understand her.

She is the river
upon whose separate banks my father and I appear,
mouthing the words to a standard tragedy.

During the day, I walk with ghosts—
all women, all ages,
all her.
She is everywhere.

Where is she?

4.

In wood, in vault, in Baltimore.

Please omit flowers.

They say it will be a cold winter, colder than last.

I have her coat.

A Quartz Contentment

Then the moment
slips away from you, an unanswered prayer.
At his wedding, your father takes you aside,
throws his heavy arm across your shoulder,
tells you everything he thinks you want to know:
I'll never love like that again, but . . .

A year ago, from Nevada,
you called your radioactive mother,
came home in time
to watch her turn blue at the ends and die.
Now, back in New York,
the telephone rings

and you stop imagining
for a moment
the novel of grief and redemption
you should have written last year,
or the year before.

It was all right, it
was lovely, you tell your friends who predicted
depression, or the black tongue of anger,
but nothing like this cool breeze,
this clean page
of nothing.

Letting Go

1. I Lie Awake Listening to Ken's Breathing

For weeks, my heart has been camping out.
He shifts, the down quilt slides
across our bodies, we curve into one another.
Dear friend, sleep-as-conversation,
witness.

2. The Father Goes Out on Dates

In these, my father and mother are divorced.
I am an angry teenager and live
with my father.
I visit my mother.
We sit at an unfamiliar table, maple,
and of Shaker simplicity.
(Our hands are the same. They are her hands.)
Outside the window, trees.

At first, I am worried:
how can she go on alone?
Soon I realize she is happy without him, without us.

3. The Father Remarries

And then there is the night toward which all nights
have been leaning.

She comes back.

We all sit in a small room,
chattering, nervous.
Sara kisses my father.
My mother lowers her eyes.
Her lashes are dark, soft, almost wet.
She who all her life angered me by obsequiousness
stuns me now with this gesture.

4.   If We Could Speak to Death, What Would We Say?

(I have come to His press conference, or
He is a guest on a TV talk show.
There are questions from the audience.)

There is so much I want to say:

that death is political;
it is necessary;
it is unnecessary;
that it follows me all the days of my life;
that it is my life;
> I eat it,
> I drink it,
> I breathe it,
I dream and undream it;
that it is the unspeakable space between myself and others;
and it is the plush black cushion, like velvet,
upon which we all rest;

that we have infringed too far on God's authority
and this is His last remaining power over us;

that there is no God:
         that the sun rises in Cancer,
             I wake from Cancer,
             I brush my Cancer,
             I wash my Cancer,
             I take off my Cancer and put on my Cancer,
             I kiss my Cancer,
             I meet my friends in Cancer,
         that the sun sets in Cancer;
that through a tunnel of blue light, I hear
the silence of the dead,
and this is music;
that across a wide river, I cannot see
the shadow of myself
but know it is there, and this
is poetry:
             not beauty, not order, not burden, not legislation, but
             consciousness,
             the dream of dreams,
             the only connection between fathers and daughters,
             generations,
             the woman rocking you to sleep
             and the woman who sleeps.

(I say: *How is my mother? Does she need anything?*)

Joan Called

Joan called. Her mother was dying.
We met at Penn Station,
trained it to Orange.
To her mother's house. Of course,
her mother wasn't there, but
her sister was. Joan, Susan,
and I sat in the kitchen
drinking tea.

My mother died in '78,
so I've got experience.
That last night, her breathing
was ragged, awful.
I got some blankets,
camped out on the wildflowered chaise longue
in my parents' bedroom.
I'd like to think
I never slept, that about midnight
I saw my father blink,
his eyes fill with tears,
and he saw mine.

If you looked in the window
of Joan's mother's house,
you'd have seen three women drinking tea.
Two of them listening to this story. Just a story.
Because my father and I could not see one another across the
    darkness
and my mother died the next morning at 8:41,
sun streaming in the window.

I'll never see Joan's face again the way
it was that night: it's the one we think
we'll wear when our mother dies.

But when that moment comes,
we wear another.

Children of tea growing cool
in darkening kitchens, we have nothing
to say to one another.
But talk is the only thing
that keeps us human.
So we keep our voices going
like a heartbeat, like the clock
ticking, so that when someone says
she's gone,
it sounds almost familiar, almost fair.

Tuscarora

Everything shifts: orange hills,
pale hills, Nevada hills.
Everything shifts into valleys
of light. . . .

Morning interrupts the night.
A fragment from the diary of a woman artist:
Again, I feel as I used to when the children were sick.
I stayed closely by them, did everything for them,
did not even think about my own work.
Tending them back to health.
This glorious feeling then of reconquest:
they will stay,
I shall keep them.

I hold a young goat in my arms.
Her thin, crooked legs,
like broken pencils, twitch
and beg for the ground.
Released, she runs back to the shed,
graceful again,
the dry earth echoing beneath her hooves.
I feel the vibration in my toes.

My father walked forever down a hall,
to me, forever waiting by a nurses' station.
What is it, I said.
They can't save your mother
and he fell into my arms and I
into his Oh Dad, oh Dad, and together
we sailed away
while upstairs in surgery
woman overboard the doctors called a year too late.

Hills, valleys, invisible ocean . . .
The sun sets a hundred different ways behind this ghost town.
Sick moon rises, drips
like a candle into me;
I harden like wax.

I think of children leaning forward with warm, empty breasts,
tending to death those they could not tend to health,
those who could not stay, all the mothers
we could not keep.

Switzerland or Somewhere

It didn't matter. Wherever
they went so my father could get
away from the phone. Soon, the postcards:
"So beautiful here. Wish you could see.
You'd want to write a poem. . . ."

Oh, Mom, I'm not interested in beauty:
your lakes sparkling like champagne,
your views, always "breathtaking"; and what kind of person,
I ask my friends, types out names and addresses
on self-sticking labels *before* the vacation?

I'm not interested in beauty, my feet stamp
out in teenage disgust and freedom
through the empty house. (Two weeks
every August I reveled in orphanhood.)
It's a lie,
it's the deception you've wrapped us in,
like rubber tape around a sizzling wire.
Look at me. There's nothing beautiful about me,
except perhaps a bit around the eyes:

deep-set, brown, resisting adornment. What I'm after
is terrible:
an end to silence, or
absolute silence, and
nothing
in between.
Read me. You won't find
your silver pools,
your landscapes trembling with units of snow.

No, Mom, I'm not interested in beauty.
And when you lie,

finally still, your chest a quiet, loosened field beneath which
death rests too,
would you, if you could, write:
"So beautiful here. Wish you could see.
You'd want to write a poem. . . ."

Is this why you don't come back?
Cancer ate your tongue,
festered your inner cheeks,
turned your teeth black, your breath foul,
sucked your gums to crusted sores.
I asked, *Does it hurt?* but never, *Let me see.*
Oh but Mom, you can come back now. I promise you:
I'm a poet; I'm not interested in beauty.

Family Happiness

1.

We were in mourning for my mother, who had died in the autumn.
Black suited me.

My poor friends!—glued to my stories like a studio audience
to their cues: cards with black borders flashing **cry, applaud,**

sigh. By Thanksgiving Day,
I'd ripped a telephone book to falling leaves,

and married in the spring a good man who knew her vaguely
but not well enough, guaranteed, to ever say:

"You're just like her." Once my father, tyrannical seer,
sputtered, "You'll be divorced by the time you're thirty."

This wasn't nice. Truth is, he loved my mother like a maniac;
it tore the breath out of me when he tugged the wedding ring

from her lifeless finger. But *till death do us part.*
We all go to the grave single. For the divorce,

I dressed her in a silk pantsuit (forgive me, it was the '70s),
and obsessed: would she want to be wearing a bra? Anyway,

it's five years now, and I never say, "If only she were here."
But it's strange, at dinners, at lulls in the conversation,

the words *my mother* form inside my mouth
and long to be said to strangers.

2.

What is it about birds? I don't know a robin from
a freckle-speckled soothsayer. All the best poets

today are skilled storytellers specializing
in abstract characters with concrete perceptions.

For instance, a young woman dressed in black
leans on her windowsill. She has call-waiting

so her line is never busy. She's been married
five years with only one affair. She notices

things: this painting is like that feeling
which is like that person who best expressed

a certain idea. What is it about birds? In a flock,
they seem to be of one mind,

and goal-oriented in a preoccupied way. They
don't interest her, but they're convenient,

like certain words: *dreams, chisel, ululate,*
still, and *sorry, I lost something in my computer.*

What is it about birds? They're convenient,
inaccessible, and generally small. She's sorry

about that affair; it was inevitable, but still
she's sorry. And when she told a friend

she'd had an affair with so-and-so, she felt
immediately guilty, not so much about the thing

itself, but the choice of words; felt worse too
as she suddenly knew there are so few

choices in terms of words and therefore in terms
of action. That's why so many people at the funeral

wore blue. Because you're supposed to wear black,
but why? We don't have to do everything we're

supposed to, but blue is pretty close to black,
just to be sure. And when you think about the way

her father looked, the things he said, the way
she looked at him, the things they didn't say,

the whole scene in all its idiosyncratic
familiarity, you think, of course: birds.

3.

Suddenly, everyone's turning the age their mothers were
when they were born. We notice this

and get weird anyway.
Like the other day,

a couple in a bookstore.
Suddenly, he was angry, she was repentant. Or

the other way around. It's pretty much always
like that; some tiny, nothing of a little thing

that's everything: indicative, meaningful,
symptomatic. By the way, the only thing she does better than him

is swim. He hits the water and sinks:
this seems a personal insult. On the other hand, it's clear

they love one another. Otherwise,
why buy bookshelves, or invest in seaside holidays?

No, it's more than that. Let's say before they were married
she read a certain story, and cried at the end,

when the young wife gives up her dreams of something, or
    someone,
different, for the something and someone

she has. Let's say she knew she wasn't supposed to weep;
knew the writer was telling her those weren't dreams,

they were illusions. But that's always been
a difficult distinction. So when she sees that book again,

with a different cover, a watercolor, small stains of blue,
possibly birds?—suddenly unsure

but desperate, she wants a whole series of things that most
people want. She wants wisdom, grace, maybe even babies,

but in a different context,
you understand, than most people want them.

Most of all, she wants the passion
of relief. So that she can lie down on a sheet of sand,

watch with equanimity and only mild derangement
the young girls in their young skin playing footsie with the ocean,

the old women in their stately glide to the water's edge.
So that she can reach over, touch the wrist of the man she chose
    years

ago, and with the other hand leisurely turn the pages of a story
she knows won't make her cry anymore.

III

Baltimore

Baltimore

1.

Never write anything, my father warned me,
you'd be embarrassed to see
as the headline story in *The Baltimore Sun.*

2.

Dear Editor:
The end of the day is two blue chairs,
two cold, golden glasses.

The child's had her nap, her usual dream:
someone, something, turning the knob—

and she wakes—
angry,
to the comfortable poison of their voices
below. Down the stairs, two at a time,
with her milk-bottle bank,
to the landing,

where she shatters into blood and pennies.

Face down; inhale:
wet wool, broken glass.

Listen: screams.

3.

My father always wore a suit
at the dinner table, always
stained his tie, barked
Damn! and blamed it

on our cook, or my sweetly-
crocked mother.

But love? Oh yes, there
was love. My father loved
my mother, and my mother
loved her husband
and her children,
and the children
loved the cook,
and the cook
loved the children and the dog,
a long-haired german shepherd
dark as a wolf, neurotic
as a poet.

4.

Rich was right about Dickinson:
Vesuvius at home, protecting her slant truth.
(1700 poems stitched like a wound!):
My Life had stood—a Loaded Gun—

This image shook the hands of women
who held the pen. It was always
a glimpse of a white hem they saw, always
disappearing down a narrow hall.

But I had her confused with someone else—
another girl—
equally determined and equally guilty

Lizzie Borden took an axe
And gave her Mother forty whacks

"I am in Danger, Sir—"
"You
are in Danger, Sir—"

When she saw what she had done,
She gave her Father forty-one

or even another, in a clapboard house
at the harbor's edge, bent at the waist
from her second-story window,
to the soldiers below

"Shoot, if you must, this old gray head,
But spare your country's flag," she said

Women, strolling to my edges.

5.

In Baltimore, sex and intelligence
dogged my days.
Something sullen in me grew;
something thick, wet, unladylike,
something that embarrassed
my parents' friends, trying to smile
across the vicious card table,
their drinks sweating into cork coasters.

Their children were perfect
monsters
too, but no one let on.

We all slouched. Slammed doors. Toyed
with cults and wrote a bit of nasty stuff.
Our rooms smelled funny.
We talked in code.

"Jan, when are you happy?"
the doctor asked, and, after my answer,
"Oh, but you don't get to do *that* very often, do you?"

6.

Of course there was Whitman:

If I worship any particular thing, it shall be some of the spread of
   my body

Of course there was maple and wheat and sweaty brooks and
   dews and

wind whose soft-tickling genitals rub against me it shall be you

But how to put the above into practice
in Baltimore

where beads of lust harden like rabbit pellets
and hit their mark with the tinny ping

we strove for in years of tennis lessons?
I went looking for wild, humid forests
and to lay myself down in green pastures

and found only the Roland Park Golf Course;
better than nothing, I clung to someone's neck

and we pounded the earth and the stars shook.
Or was it my eyes in my flapping head?

Oh, if I can't be a saint or a sinner
I think I'll grow up to be a press secretary,

and breakfast with reporters, say:
"No comment. No comment."

7.

Some cities are more interesting than others.
Baltimore is forty minutes north of Washington.

The North thinks it's South,
and the South thinks it's North,
but this really hasn't mattered since the Civil War
except to Baltimoreans,
who find it oddly pleasing to be neither too much of one thing
nor too much of another.

It's a city with some charm
and a distinguished cultural heritage:
in the hard-heaving waters of the bay,
Francis Scott Key wrote our unsingable national anthem;
Edgar Allan Poe is buried there;
Gertrude Stein studied medicine there;
Zelda Fitzgerald was institutionalized there.

You can still find a juicy corned-beef sandwich
on Lombard Street, and a cup of tea and something like scones
in the lunchroom of the Women's Exchange;
even the most respectable of families will chug and holler
for the Colts and pry
and suck steaming crabs to steaming smithereens.

Four Baltimoreans signed the Declaration of Independence.
(*Samuel Chase*d *Paca* with a *Stone*. . . .)
They're streets now,
lined with burnt-brick semidetacheds
shaded by maples
(I was mugged on Chase),
and you've probably heard of the neat, three-tiered
marble steps that the proud women of Baltimore
scrub every Sunday morning,
or used to.

The sun rises with a kind of mastery
over the suburbs, where the schools are better and dogs
named after Roman emperors run free.

8.

And that sky like butter, those kisses like butter.
I used to race around a grand dining-room table
popping those scalloped balls into my mouth:
sweet marbles. And then retire to my playroom
to learn all the possible combinations of color:

summer nights, until my childhood was over,
the city fathers illuminated the lonely fountain
in Druid Hill Lake: pink then yellow, yellow
then blue; blue then misty green, then silver,
then yellow, then pinky blue, then misty red, then . . .

9.

My brother wants the bookcase,
so I'll take the piano. He doesn't play.
He calls me up two weeks in advance
to warn, the truck may be too small.
I say, we'll cross that bridge . . .
You know the rest.

This isn't death.
A house becomes its parts easily enough.
At least this one does.
Strangers finger my grandmother's dolls,
haggle over the mattress
on which I became a woman.

My mother doesn't know, remains firm.
"You know what that costs new?"
She gets her price. My secret
is strapped to the top of a Ford
and whisked away.
Books move more slowly. A woman

taps the binding of *Being and Nothingness,*
turns aside. I slide it

off the shelf and into my bag. Later,
we'll pack the things our future
is made of, but now we're selling
the past, and I'm the one—

the prophet of this family!—

clinging to broken tie-racks
and costume jewelry.
"Jan, we never knew you cared—"
I don't! I don't! But couldn't someone
stop this, just for a moment?
Let one chip in a wine glass
remind us how it broke? Someone

would be grateful
for even a cliché: this shell,
this husk, this place,
this awful place;
some reason for moving,
some pain to relocate.

10.

Now why don't you write something cheerful,
something shadowless and inspiring,
something about honeysuckle,
its open-mouthed baby kisses,
the way it swept the alleys of Baltimore
in a lazy, extravagant announcement of Spring?

Why don't you write about
the spaceships on your bedroom wall
in the years of the peaceful atom?
Or 4th of July at Lystra Meadows?
Or those summers in Maine, sticky pinecones
scattered across the beach?

Or the first time you met anybody?
How perfect he was! He used to make up songs
as he drove you home: *I love Jan's nose,
it grows and grows.* . . .
He loved the whole long length of you
for a while; life wasn't so bad.

It was really rather nice, sometimes,
wasn't it? Eisenhower, then Kennedy,
then those beautiful May days: cherry blossoms
and petitions. And why not say
something about the soft, soft skin
of your breasts? Those were the days:

sex wasn't always a weeping willow.
Let's face it: you looked great
in your yellow bathing suit
with the lacy trim;
you were the most popular girl at camp;
you slept with every man you wanted to;
you read Simone de Beauvoir

and knew how to put everything into perspective.
So now you could, if you tried,
write about honeysuckle.
You could. You could.

II.

Okay. Hot coffee. My mother sets up a bean-grinding
Vesuvian roar that shakes the springs in my bed.
Who can sleep with a family in the house?

I take the stairs two at a time,
meet Caesar at the door,
pry the morning paper from his slobbery jaw,

kiss my mother's buttery skin,
my father's bald head, cold as marble.
My brother disappears, the door flapping behind him.

The Baltimore Sun opens like smithereens.
All our secrets have made the front page.
In every home in this tenth-largest city,

delight and horror. Oh, look here, it says
he never really loved her, or if he did,
never enough, and *this* is what she thinks of us—

and my father's eyes turn from blue to gray, then gray to black,
    then
black in a circle of pink:

"Oh, was it really like that?"
and, in all honesty,

(oh our tears, our tears, our honeysuckle tears)—

I can't answer.

IV

This Place

There is the poetry of obsession and the poetry of invitation.
There is the moment you say *come,* and the moment you say
   welcome.
There is happiness, there is despair.
When I was seven, Lisa, my maybe-Sullivanian soul mate, asked:
Where does the sky end?
We lay side-by-side on the grass, comfortable as sleepers,
and strained our eyes to see:
There! No, there!

Her brother, Nicky, short and lean,
is a jockey now, straddling the sleek, sweating beauties of Pimlico.
My brother, who tickled us both into sex,
lives in Westport with his wife and four bedrooms.
But what happened to Lisa?
She turned red and sniffly in her mother's blond arms
though I promised always to love her,
though I promised nothing would change,

Everything changed.
Debby Rothman's hula skirt teased a jack-o'-lantern
till her limbs turned charcoal; Robby stole his father's car
and hit the brakes too late.

And we moved away and away and away.

There is our childhood and there is our youth,
there are our fathers, constant and disinterested as the sun,
there is happiness and there is something wilder than happiness.
When I was nine, I first felt the swell and pull of the ocean:
   Impossible,
my mother said, you can never see the other side.
But I saw Russia in full imperial splendor, a mistier line of blue
   just past the blue.
There! No, there!

Now there are the people we admire,
waving to us, or to one another: Karl Marx throws off his glasses,
slams shut his books, strides out of the British Museum
to embrace Frank O'Hara; Charles Bukowski and Emma Goldman
share the same passion-tossed sheets;
Amelia Earhart swims to shore, her long strong legs
glisten with salt; Anne Frank's toeprints
disappearing teaspoons as she races down to meet her.
There is heaven, a vast library,
the soft murmur more thrilling than life.

And there is this day,

so cold, so warm, so utterly without direction or likeness.
The sun rose at 5:43, the snow blue as oil, small birds careened.
When I am tired and lonely, I come to this place
to be more alone.
But I set my simple table,
two chipped goblets,
wine of patient vintage,
and watch through the window, day and night,
for all that I've lost, or thought I've lost,
come home to me.
There! No, there!

Get This

I did not get this from any book
I got this from cornfields washed out, waved
out under racing moon
splitting like brain
Right side right side right side
Left side left side left side

I did not get this from any book
but from tongue of dog
wide, pink as my tongue
long as I live lick lasts
and love is something brown-eyed, drowsy
I got this from sleep, I got this from waking
I would have traded for sleep, waking
long after nights of purpled sky
nippled with clouds

I did not get this from any book
I got this on trust and betrayal, I got this on trust
I got this on trust funds
on loan
with interest
I got this from inhale inhale inhale
exhale exhale exhale

I did not get this from blood, blood
means nothing, I did not get this from nature
or nurture, I did not get this from any book

I got this from mind that muscles
outmuscles heart
I got this from hangnail
from hangman
from hanging above a rushing river

this bank roaring
that bank roaring

I got this from mushrooms, I got this from sitting at the table
late later later and still I would not eat

I got this from leaves and spine
I got this from stranger who said I want
to take your picture, come here, come
back here, drop your blouse from your shoulder
lower a little lower a little lower

I got this from necklines
standing on lines, sign on the dotted lines
I got this from scissors
but I was always losing the scissors
I got this from A my name is
B my name is
I got this from scissors, but I was always losing the scissors
I got this from rock, I got this from rock
and roll all the world over so easy to see
people everywhere just gotta be

I got this from paper, please listen to me
but I did not get this from any book
understand me now I did not get this from any book
I got this from light on the books at 1, 2, 3 in the morning
the whole house so quiet it could have been dead
I could have been the only one even trying to live but I did
not get this from any book

even when I danced at 4 in the morning
even when I wept at 5 in the morning
even when I danced, even when I wept
look, here's the path traveled from eye to mouth
first tear
second tear

call a life an open book I did not get this from any book
call a life a closed book I did not get this from any book
call may God inscribe your name in the book of life
I did not get this from any book come into my library
said the spider to the fly
open any book
it will tell you I did not get this from it
even if I burn it I will have this
even if I burn it
even if I burn

Not Bad, Dad, Not Bad

I think you are most yourself when you're swimming;
slicing the water with each stroke,
the funny way you breathe, your mouth cocked
as though you're yawning.

You're neither fantastic nor miserable
at getting from here to there.
You wouldn't win any medals, Dad,
but you wouldn't drown.

I think how different everything might have been
had I judged your loving
like I judge your sidestroke, your butterfly,
your Australian crawl.

But I always thought I was drowning
in that icy ocean between us,
I always thought you were moving too slowly to save me,
when you were moving as fast as you can.

Moonstone

Someday, they'll make a movie of us,
honey. Then, even this will look good:
our one room, our single sooty window,
even our kitchen, with its sink
so narrow one night it took both of us
to wedge our salad bowl out of it.
Even our dust-colored carpet,
not what we wanted at all, we wanted Moonstone
but Moonstone was out of our
ballpark, besides,
we had to be practical, Moonstone
was too pale and shimmery, within a week
it would show its stains.

Someday, they'll make a movie of us, honey.
You'll come in the door after work.
I'm waiting up for you, reading. When we squeeze
into the bathroom to brush our teeth, I'm not
whining about my gums receding, you're not
complaining about the tire around your waist.
We just have all this white foam,
like whipped cream, around our mouths,
and we're laughing, and a little
speck or two of white
sails onto the camera lens.

When they make that movie of us, honey, our whole lives,
cut, condensed to instruct,
will shimmer.

Yes, even this gray and ordinary room will shimmer.

Even this week.

Even this whole year.

Even the last eleven years, when it seemed to us nothing
was happening.

Yes, even this gray, ordinary carpet
will shimmer.

Fact is, you've just dragged in from work.
You're tired, beaten down. I'm waiting up
for you, bored and stupid from the book
I'm supposed to be reading. I pat
a place beside me. Come here, honey.
We sit, facing one another,
on our dust-colored carpet—not
what we wanted at all, not us
at all—and we talk.
Late into the night, we talk.
We sit on our gray, dust-colored carpet, late into the night,
and we talk.

Moonstone.

Rome

1. The Forum

The guidebooks tell more than we need to know:
every shadow, every mindless column
conquered.

But oh my dear we are small here.
Uninformed and alone.
Across the path,
you squint into the sun,
stain your fingers charcoal
to sketch some history
we cannot understand.

You love everything
old and solid.
How does it last?

2. The Gallery

Napoleon's sister was bored
and Canova's studio warm:
now every tourist leers at her marble breasts.

We're in a Cardinal's whorehouse, husband,
where even the frescoed angels cheat on God.
Each painting tells a dirty joke,
but we're not laughing.

Outside, we peel and share
a swollen grapefruit,
count our money,
count the days gone and the days left.

3. The Chapel

Today the ruins cry out
hold fast.
Our clasped hands loosen.

We follow a long wall, like soldiers
in search of the sublime.

Finally, above our raised heads,
Adam's casual fingers . . .

4.

It was never supposed to be in Rome,
not in this small room,
not now. We were going to grow old
before this happened; we were going to invent
a new, intractable love;
we were going to change,
or die, but never this:

votive candles for sex,
wine tasting of cork,
your kisses too soft tonight,
too familiar.

Marriage

1.

The painter
paints.

Inside the body,
a mind.
Inside the mind,
a hand.
Inside the hand,
a brush.

You have loved him for what seems
all your life.

2.

One morning.
Dogwood's wet mouth to your window.

The night before,
in a cold car,
you held him while he cried. The heart does break.

You can see it in a man's shoulders.
They go up and down, up and down.

3.

A man's head curled into his pillow.
Swirls and eddies of his hair.
His beard bravely growing into the morning.

The plots of our lives do not match their themes.
I left him, I came back. Does this mean
I never really left at all?

4.

I left you. It was a Sunday. Or a Monday. I was the wind
all day.

5.

No use. Even now, the beginning and end
fit together, but the middle falls out.
And we fall in.

6.

And that scratching? Did I mention that scratching
at our door? It assumes the shape of another man,
but there's no need to be specific. No need to be
specific about his hair. Yellow-white. Or his eyes.
Blue. Or how long I'd known him. Years.

7.

The painter
paints.

Inside the body,
a mind.
Inside the mind,
a hand.
Inside the hand,
a brush.
Or a knife.

A palette knife to get the surface he wants:

he wants
history.
You only
get that
with a knife.

He wants
his wife
to come back.

She does.
She comes to see the painting.
She loves it,
though she wishes
there were more
yellow, white,
or blue,
she's not sure.

Walking to their car, she tells him,
We knew one another
in many other lives.

We saw one another often
from different windows of the palace.

8.

All I really want to tell you
is that the heart does break.
You can see it in a man's shoulders.

Marriage 2

One morning. I remember. My eyes steady, impartial.
I remember the individual dogwood blossoms,

the lazy ones, the eager; the drone
of a refrigerator; a windowshade's worrying tongue.

I could tell you how many dark bills were curled on our dresser,
even the dates of the brown pennies, still

warm from last night's palms. One morning, that morning,
the earth opened up. We fell into that gaping fissure. We kept

falling. I plunged past the ledge where the potion that said *husband,
drink me,* gleamed. This happened, was

happening, kept happening. I had just woken up, you
were about to, and me, pitched up on one elbow.

My God. What is more lovely than a man's head, curled
into his pillow? The swirls and eddies of his hair? His beard silently

growing into the morning? And what is more terrifying than your
love for him? All this happened. I heard a scratching at the door,
was I so

wrong to think someone was coming to deliver me another life,
my real one? Was I so wrong to think when something dies,
something else

is born? The plots of our lives do not match their themes. I left
you, I came back. Does this mean I might as well have never left

at all? Even now when I tell this story, the beginning and end
fit together, but the middle falls out. And that scratching?

Remember those 19th-century novels? Destiny used
to be so grand, so tragically instructive. Now, it comes nosing

its way into our bedrooms like a stupid puppy
to settle across our warm feet and teach us nothing.

Just as That Night

This train is rocking me to you,
rocking me home. They say
that when our mothers die, we go
looking for another, that the soul,
like a body, adjusts to
loss, that women
trade sex for touch. Lover
whom I barely know and
cannot know, when you throw
me against the wall and slap against
me oh and oh God what I
want is happening but what I need
cannot be touched or calmed
or quelled; just as that night
so long ago and so clear to me,
when I wept and called
out for her, she came,
stepping through the wall
like a white nylon ghost, but still
could not warm me
enough or make me believe tomorrow
the world would not go
dark again and empty of her.
Of course
now I know
it's not anger or disdain that soothes you
into sleep while I
lie twitching
for some declaration
even the most loving eyes
cannot sign. But still all my
life it's that dream,
that waking from dream,

that rocks me into and out of men's arms:
Lover, walk through walls for me,
walk through that wall.

Halfway

I'm standing beneath a tree now,
a lazy-branched birch near a house
by a river. Through rustling light
and dark, a man and woman inside.

This is how I see them: he,
standing before his painting,
palette knife in hand drenched
in yellow; she, close beside.

Though I can't hear her words,
I know by the radiant curve
of his attention, she's telling him
his picture is halfway there.

When he's finished his painting,
he'll call it *Halfway Where*.
Halfway where, darlings of any
gender, isn't that a long way

to travel together? I'm moving
away from this tree by the river.
As I go, this is how I want
to keep us: blessing these woods

we lost one another in, blessing
these trees, even their dying leaves,
and their dying color, yellow.
A sweet yellow. Tender, if

you'll let me use that word.
Please, for all of us who once
had a love, and now have another,
let us use that word tender, tenderly.

This One's for You

Even if you didn't have green eyes (in the bathtub, blue).
Even if you didn't have a lovely singing voice,
    or care for Alexandrine champagne
    some slow Saturday evenings to sing it through,
it pleases me, your lips close to my ear,
    or when you're a big girl, and I'm a big girl too.

Five years difference between we two.
Sometimes it hardly matters. I've decided to worship you,
    Diana, goddess of the forest—
    or is she the one of the hunt?
    Who cares? You remind me of her
too. Some woman caught me up, breathless, in her strong arms,
    said *breathe, darling.* Her eyes were green-blue.

Vague resemblances: that's the daily news.
Meaning: I'm willingly a fool for you
    any hour past midnight,
    and almost anytime in three-quarter view.
    Consider this, too: stumbling back, after a fight,
to someplace we could call home, you and I have been known
    to duet a jubilee so funky it sounds like the blues.

What steady arrows you shoot, Diana, become
a goddess of the hearth: you whisper
    time to put the porchlight on,
    and we do. Who am I talking to?
What is this strange glare, this prescience that you won't be true?
Sometimes you say something like *even so, boo,*
and it sounds like *breathe, darling.* That's why this one's for you.

Waiting for This Story to End
Before I Begin Another

All my stories are about being left,
all yours about leaving. So we should have known.
Should have known to leave well enough alone;
we knew, and we didn't. You said let's put
our cards on the table, your card
was your body, the table my bed, where we didn't
get till 4 am, so tired from wanting
what we shouldn't that when we finally found our heads,
we'd lost our minds. *Love*, I wanted to call you
so fast. But so slow you could taste each
letter licked into your particular and rose-like ear.
L, love, for let's wait. *O,* for oh no, let's not. *V*
for the precious v between your deep breasts
(and the virtue of your fingers
in the voluptuous center of me.)

Okay, *E* for enough.

Dawn broke, or shattered. Once we've made
the promises, it's hard to add the prefix *if.* . . .
But not so wrong to try.
That means taking a lot of walks,
which neither of us is good at,
for different reasons, and nights up till 2
arguing whose reasons are better.
Time and numbers count a lot in this. 13
years my marriage. 5 years you my friend.
4th of July weekend when something that begins
in mist, by mistake (whose?), means too much
has to end. I think we need an abacus to get our love
on course, and one of us to oil the shining rods
so we can keep the crazy beads clicking,

clicking. It wasn't a question
of a perfect fit. Theoretically,
it should be enough to say I left a man
for a woman (90% of the world is content
to leave it at that. Oh, lazy world) and when the woman
lost her nerve, I left
for greater concerns: when words like autonomy
were useful, I used them, I confess. So I get
what I deserve: a studio apartment he paid the rent on;
bookshelves up to the ceiling she drove
the screws for. And a skylight I sleep alone
beneath, and two shiny quarters in my pocket
to call one, then the other, or to call one

twice. Once, twice, I threatened to leave him—
remember? Now that I've done it, he says
he doesn't. I'm in a phonebooth at the corner of Bank
and Greenwich; not a booth, exactly,
but two sheets of glass to shiver between.
This is called being street-smart: dialing
a number that you know won't be answered,
but the message you leave leaves proof that you tried.
And this, my two dearly beloveds, is this called
hedging your bets? I fish out my other
coin, turn it over in my fingers, press
it into the slot. Hold it there. Let it drop.

Satisfaction

I once had a friend who had a friend, she said,
who smelled like crayons.
She said (my friend), I want Daniella at my funeral,

I'd know her sweet scent anywhere,
the smell of crayons in your pocket.
Now my friend is not my friend

anymore. But she's reading over my shoulder,
she's saying *that crayon line is mine!*, and it makes me
want to go back and erase it. Beethoven's

late quartets on my boom box, all watery strings,
matter-of-fact and grief-stricken.
It's possible to be both,

you know. And happy, too. For one, two, five
years, I wrote barely a word
(for six months, couldn't even address a postcard),

because I didn't want to give her
(my old friend)
the satisfaction. Then one changeable May—

every gorgeous day followed by
three or four Seasonal Affective Disorder ones—
and I could scarcely stop the words.

They tumbled out, like crayons from a pocket.
Bless everything was the month-long mood,
and it had nothing to do with love

(well, maybe a little), or lost love,
or learning from lost love. The music slows down,
we go gray and innocent waiting for it

to take us to a crucial, expected place.
It takes us someplace else entirely, then sets
like the sun.

Dear One(s)

In your book, I've receded to an s.
(Did you think I wouldn't notice? I noticed.)
I'm a trail of smoke from a cigarette you put out,
a pattern, or a trend, like the gluttonous end

of the gluttonous '80s. I don't care. Much.
Really. You can do what you like
with me, not that you need my permission.
That was a long time ago, when we were saluting

in that various field. Even my handwriting's
changed. I no longer avoid you,
nor seek you out. You're the historian,
I'm the sociologist, or the other way around,

it hardly matters. I can't even remember
your phone number, and I'm terribly fond of mine.
I can look out the window again.
I'm going to be fine. I'm fine.

VI

Tuscarora 2

Nine years after my mother died, I went back to where I was,
not when she died, but when she was dying.
Tuscarora: half a dozen shacks,

handful of Winnebagos slapped along the dusty cross
Main Street and Dynamite Boulevard make
when they cross at the boarded-up tavern,

where bartender Warren used to mix drinks with the stump
of a thumb he lost the rest to in a turquoise crusher,
circa 1947. Tuscarora: an honest-to-God

ghost town, 50 miles from the nearest real town,
but hometown to old friends Dennis and Julie,
postmodern hippies whose favorite possession's

their satellite dish: 47 channels of the same old crap
make you feel not so lonesome. Desert brown
10 shades of brown. Takes a while to get used to,

this absence of beauty that's beauty,
and visibility, on a good day, forever—
or at least Idaho. That's the state where, I once read,

if you tip the country on its side, all the nuts roll.
Therefore, somewhere over the desert hills, neo-Nazis
are plotting the next revolution, survivalists sorting

stacks of canned fruit. Today, Ken and Dennis
are wearing their otter-skin Afghanistan caps;
later this afternoon two neighbors will stop by with a blood-

drenched white bunny for dinner. Meantime,
we're climbing up past the men's dump, up past the women's,
air growing stingy in our lungs. We stop.

Dennis takes a picture. A year from now I'll find it
when Ken and I are dividing our things—
you'd think we were standing on the moon.

Tuscarora 3

Nine years after my mother died,
I went back to where I was,
not when she died, but when
she was dying. At 5 am,
Dennis comes into the house,
stomping his boots. For
the next hour, the sun slits
open the canyon, shines
across 8 cracked miles.

Everybody's mother dies,
that's not what makes me
special. We gave her
a shot at about 2 am.
A spastic crow flew
across the room,
we had to drag her
twitching body back to bed,
clean the trail of shit
she'd splattered in her flight.

Wait. I'm getting ahead
of my story, which isn't
really a story. Everybody's
mother dies; everybody
loves a twisty, turny,
forky road and winds up
looking over their shoulder
at a clean, flat line
between A and B, like
the one that stitches
us to Elko,
through 52 miles of wrinkled hills,
like the folds

of a Weimaraner sleeping
on its side.

Once I gave a poetry reading
with a folk singer. He'd
get the whole room rocking,
rolling, clapping along,
tapping their feet.
Then I'd kick in with a poem
and you've never heard
such silence.
Don't you
have any happy poems?
he wondered. Don't
you know any cancer songs?
I asked.

You have to have
a certain mind to live
in the desert. My mother
didn't care for it. She liked mountains,
lakes, Switzerland. Trees with fruit,
cute shops. When they were plugging
the radium into her mouth,
I was swimming in the mineral quarry.
Ken and I were one year
from getting married,
ten years from divorce,
that old ghost town.

The Second Movement of Anything

It was not given me
to be easily joyous:
something stands in the way,
like a screen,
like a veil,
like the unlearned names of flowers—
tuberose,
bloodroot,
false indigo,
morning glory,
whatever,
and the demented
gardener who hisses
you should know, you should know. . . .

That's why
mother's breasts tumble.
That's why this perpetual;
that's why the red
tractor
that radicalizes
the gold fields.

The second movement
of anything
is my forte.
After the hoopla,
the big splash,
the no-strings-attached
3-week cruise
to you-name-it,
after all the I'm gonna love you forevers,
the daddy finally understands
it was all a big mistake,

there's this,
well, let's call it, um,
reconsideration.

I know it like the back
of the leaf
that so many who
have held my hand
have held.
Listen, it's delicious.
Listen, it's heartbreaking.
Listen, it's an industry, for god's sake,
it's a high-level kind of sadness thing.
Listen, it's heartbreaking,
but then it's over,
just like this moment
backstabbing its way into the next.

Poem for You, Dead by Suicide

Whenever I think of you, I see my face.
Three-quarter view
in a train window. I'm trying
not to look, but I'm looking.

I'm in the train, or on
it, as we say. I've just left you
to preserve my dignity,
but I left a minute too late.

Trees, Hudson River, idiotic smokestacks
flow over my shoulder.

Years later, the last time we'll meet,
we'll also be on a train.
By chance. I'll be wearing

my green coat. Green for envy.
Green for resolute, blossom, kama and sutra.
Green for sophistication.
We're traveling in the same direction,
but you'll get off

first. Years later,
the last time we won't
meet, news of your death comes up from behind
to buckle my knees.
Dirty trick you played,
being absent for six months,
not pressing your feet

into the same earth I walk on,
which is all I asked for
really, really all I asked for.

A Day

A window in the bedroom is a photograph of a river.
Then it's a painting of a river.
Then a movie of a river.
Then a river.

Mornings are coffee on the deck. Four translations
of Rilke. Sunlight concentrates on two things:
coming and going, or coming to stay,
slithering along the lawn.

Once in a while, a canoer floats by. Very very
slowly. Enough time to trade the story
of our lives, if we wanted to.
You'd say that line was

extreme, but I'm just trying to give you a sense of how
time passes here. Slow motion is very popular
in nature. A single blade of grass could
take forever

to bend and rise up again, and we've got lots and lots of grass
here. We've also got hemlocks, river birch. Great
blue herons fly funny, their legs flapping
behind like afterthoughts.

The sunflowers don't care if I write a poem about them,
or anything for that matter. But I do. I'd like very
much to tell you how they bob and weave
in the wind when it's windy,

how they don't when it's not. Maybe if I lived here ten years I
could. There are so many different kinds
of leaves, each leaf is a different
kind of tree,

and then there are barks, and growing patterns, and a whole
lot of other things to consider before you can make
a positive identifiication. And I'm just here
for the summer.

Who knew you'd have to spend a whole life to write about
one day? I mean fairly. I mean truly. Pity
I hadn't heard that sooner,
I might have

been a doctor or a lawyer. Healed people or defended them.
Instead of running down to the river whenever
it calls me (it's turning fall here—white lips
on the water)

and waving down the next poor soul who floats my way:
Hey, you there! Yes, you! Come here!
I have something to tell you!

I walk back and forth in my room. . . .

I walk back and forth in my room,
shaking my arms and legs,
trying to shake the love out.

But it won't go. One cockeyed trillium, endangered
member of the lily family,
watches me from the windowsill—

oh silly girl, she's saying,
you plucked me
when you knew it was wrong:

did you expect no ramifications?

And Have It, Too

You grind your teeth in your sleep. I snarl. After, the luscious,
    felled sea, stained triangle of dazzle and distress,
        not quite at our feet. Shall we stand at this shelf,

this shelf we stand at the beginning of? You grind. I hurricane.
    We swam in the hurricane! Not here.
        Back there. Exciting, abnormal patterns the wind

broke the water into, melting aluminum. You grind.
    Shall I wake you? And if I should, would you tell me of the bridge
        you are building? Just one more step, just one more,

and you have crossed over to the other side. But every day,
    you're where you were the day before,
        just as far from the opposite shore. *Who is at the far shore*

is who is on this one. You grind your teeth in your sleep; I snarl.
    Imagine: to have come all this way only to report the storm
        in our minds. . . . But fact:

hurricane! hurricane!
    It tore trees from their roots, chewed up power lines.
        Two lawn chairs that had been ours spasm-skidded

across the deck. A birdhouse plunged to the earth like a suicide.
    We lost our lights, our news, our phone.
        Our waterpump died, and the toilet overflowed.

You hurricane. I hurricane. It's our nature, it's our mothers
    with their gorgeous, furious breasts, it's our fathers
        bailing out the basements of our childhoods,

that wet, sticky mess. Stop here. An hour later, the calm is divine.
    A Tiffany-palette sunset lotions the sky.
        Did hurricane leave this beauty behind, or would

it have been here anyway? You hurricane. I hurricane.
What a storm. What a life.
What a long childhood, this earth.